a sky is falling

poems

Nica Cornell

Mwanaka Media and Publishing Pvt Ltd,
Chitungwiza Zimbabwe
*
Creativity, Wisdom and Beauty

Publisher: *Mmap*
Mwanaka Media and Publishing Pvt Ltd
24 Svosve Road, Zengeza 1
Chitungwiza Zimbabwe
mwanaka@yahoo.com
mwanaka13@gmail.com
https://www.mmapublishing.org
www.africanbookscollective.com/publishers/mwanaka-media-and-publishing
https://facebook.com/MwanakaMediaAndPublishing/

Distributed in and outside N. America by African Books Collective
orders@africanbookscollective.com
www.africanbookscollective.com

ISBN: 978-1-77931-489-5
EAN: 9781779314895

DISCLAIMER
All views expressed in this publication are those of the author and
do not necessarily reflect the views of *Mmap*.

Contents

Acknowledgements..vi
Preface..vii
Where I Write...1
Vallei van Verlatenheid...4
Thirteenth...5
National University Shutdown, South Africa, October 2015...........6
Confession...7
Another Suitcase, Another Hall..9
Blow-up Doll...10
Seashells...11
Characters in a Psychologist's Waiting Room................................12
Homecoming...13
Whim...14
Granny Be(a)..15
Ewe...17
Please...18
CJR...19
They have a Dream..20
Oxford..21
Institutions of Higher Education..23
You are a Colour...25
Grace..27
Fish..28
Milkbox Tray...29
Original Sin...30
Shades of Orange..31
October's Birmingham...32
Disability Advice...33
Virus 2.0...34
The Lancing...35
Modern Medicine..36
How...37

First Friend...38
Oshivambo Patsy Cline.................................39
Thirst...40
Like Riding a Bike....................................41
Accra...42
First Daughter..44
Staying Alive...45
A Political Country...................................48
Humanity..49
Written & Performed in *Ukuphuthelwa (Insomnia)*......50
Autobiography...51
Desdemona's Toothbrush................................54
Pandora...55
Travelling with Kapuscinski...........................56
What's That?..59
A Cheap Pink Ring Box.................................63
In-hail...70
Men...71
He Left me by the Hand................................72
A Love Poem...74
Once..75
Diagnosis...76
Friday's Absence......................................77
Fifteenth...78
The Spring..80
The Hysterical Girl...................................81
From One Ward Patient to Another......................82
Hands...83
Nursing...84
See Jane Run..85
In Response to Japan Pumps Seawater into Nuclear Reactor
Unit..86
The Second Election...................................88

Three Weeks...89
22...90
A Year Ago...91
Rusted Pride...95
Two Geese..98
The Secret of this Loving.........................100
Mmap New African Poets Series................102

Acknowledgements

Vallei van Verlatenheid, *Better Than Starbucks* (2022)
Thirteenth, *20.35 Africa: An Anthology of Contemporary Poetry* (2018)
National University Shutdown, South Africa, October 2015, *Botsotso 18: Poetry from Public and Private Places* (2018)
Confession, *Best New African Poets 2020 Anthology* (2021)
Seashells, *Botsotso 18: Poetry from Public and Private Places* (2018)
Characters in a Psychologist's Waiting Room, *Botsotso 18: Poetry from Public and Private Places* (2018)
Granny Be(a), *Writing Grandmothers: Africa vs Latin America Volume 2* (2019)
CJR, *Best New African Poets Anthology 2019* (2020)
They Have a Dream, *Best New African Poets Anthology 2019* (2020)
Grace, *Libero America* (2020)
Milkbox Tray, *Taint Taint Magazine* (2021)
Original Sin, *Best New African Poets Anthology 2019* (2020)
Virus 2.0, *Taint Taint Magazine* (2021)
How, *Taint Taint Taint Magazine* (2021)
First Friend, *Best New African Poets 2020 Anthology* (2021)
Oshivambo Patsy Cline, *Libero America* (2020)
Thirst, *Botsotso 18: Poetry from Public and Private Places* (2018)
Like Riding a Bike, *Kalahari Review* (2018)
Accra, *Kalahari Review* (2018)
First Daughter, *Kalahari Review* (2018)
Staying Alive, *Kalahari Review* (2018)
A Political Country, *Mobius: The Journal of Social Change* (2017)
Humanity, *The Good Men Project* (2014)
Written & Performed in *Ukuphuthelwa (Insomnia), Aerial 2012* (2012)
Autobiography, *Aerial 2012* (2012)
Desdemona's Toothbrush, *Aerial 2012* (2012)
Travelling with Kapuscinski, *Taint Taint Taint Magazine* (2021)
Two Geese, *Fixing Earth: Africa, UK & Ireland Writers Anthology Volume 2* (2022)

Preface

a sky is falling is a spare, but lyrical and original exploration of embodied experience. The poems in this collection are filled with bodies – speaking and signifying bodies; bodies endowed with meaning; bodies treated as kernels of human identity. Cornell's poetry engages directly with human experience in the corporeal: in the sensory connections of a person with the world as experienced through hearing, seeing, tasting, touching, and smelling.

Early in the collection, the poem "Thirteenth" begins as an invitation to notice sensations that are alive in the body:

> *"Go slow-ly next time*
>
> *you are inside of me*
>
> *I am fragile, a deer*
>
> *of woven glass."*

Palpable in energy, yet gentle in rhythm – the poem is representative of the collection in its entirety. It asks: how do we live with our human fragility? This question is answered through the body, which includes and constitutes its own meaning.

The idea of embodiment as a means to knowledge is expressed, again, in the poem "(W)him", wherein the utterances of the body are recorded through pain. The speaker writes: "I am the tooth you tongue/ testing the stretch of the ache." The body here, in a state of pain, represents a type of auto-signifying voice, it speaks its own strange language. This is true too in the poem, "Please". Cornell amplifies the body's pain, intent on translating its physicality to the reader:

"beneath my breasts that have swollen

to meet terror again,

to gently place your extraordinary eyes on

the spectacle

of

the groaning, lost

organ of me

dragging my weighty, shuddering body"

Suffering is the discourse of the body; it is described in terms of its own immediacy, without hindrance. This focus on corporeal pain gestures to the process of coping with trauma — a task faced by many of the bodies in the collection, specifically those bodies that belong to women.

In "Original Sin", we understand that women's bodies are the sites at which and on which control is most frequently exercised:

"Sometimes I believe them

when they tell me

I am paying the price

for my body's sin,

that men are simply ravenous –

Why else are they eating us whole?"

Here, as throughout the book, the body exists within the inscription of the social, a means of viewing the politicised world. Bartky, in her essay *Psychological Oppression* (2006), observes that the woman's body determines the identity of a woman in society. Cornell employs a post-colonial, feminist lens to reveal the heteropatriarchal capitalist bodily politics that impose themselves on what women feel and desire. It controls territories and bodies, with violence and militarisation, and inflicts punishments against those who don't conform to the norm.

In the poem "CJR", an indictment of the infamous colonialist – Cecil John Rhodes – who "[t]hey say…didn't like women", the speaker illustrates how discourses of gender, sexuality and nationalism intersect in disciplining women's bodies. The speaker reflects that they've "known his name longer than [they've] known it was one", calling for renewed attention to the impact of historical master narratives on the lives of women and a more careful examination of the influence of historical contexts on the ideological production of notions about women and their bodies.

Many of the women's' bodies in *a sky is falling* are affected by a negative body image and eating disturbances brought on by heteropatriarchal body-policing. They experience constant body monitoring – as is evinced in "Modern Medicine":

"The nurse whistles through her teeth,

tells me to stop eating

when I tell her my weight

(I've just left the psych ward,

not for my recalcitrant eating disorder.)"

In a world of commodification of women's bodies and sexualities, women's bodies want to disappear themselves and disavow their own presences, as in the penultimate lines of "You are a colour":

> *"Forgive me.*
> *Forgive the truth.*
> *I am never casual.*
> *I am never small.*
> *I am never light.*
> *I am always all."*

Yet, the bodies in *a sky is falling* resist inscription too. In "CJR," the speaker continues:

> *"Before they put the wires in,*
>
> *whenever I close my mouth (often)*
>
> *my bottom teeth dig small troughs in His gums"*

Here, the textualized body refuses violence. The speaker bites back, digging "small troughs in His gums." The capitalised "Him" may be the colonialist, history, or the patriarchy. The body becomes a destabilising force, resisting inscription, even while silent (silenced) – it finds a way to announce its presence, primacy, and power.

There are countless poets of the body, but in Cornell's hands women's bodies bleed, and leak and ache, they become sites of explicit corporeal information so that we cannot ignore them. They are "never small, never light, always all" – brought to the forefront, not as palatable or acceptable, but as an act of confrontation and resistance.

-   Sarah Lubala

Where I Write

I write at a desk bought from a charity shop named for Princess Alice. It's made of wood, painted white with blue drawers. On it sits a chipped Winnie The Pooh mug of pens and a roll-up crayon or two. There's a neat tower of Roald Dahl themed mini suitcases, holding pages, kokis and make-up. It holds in place a calendar with a different piece of vintage fashion for each day of the year. Each month has its own colour. We're Purple at present – the colour that condemned Thomas Cromwell to the executioner in Hilary Mantel's The Mirror and the Light. Beside me is a mannequin named Nicolette. My husband and I take turns dressing her for our moods and that of the flat. She is currently wearing an imitation vintage salmon sleeveless dress, with a matching mohair shawl that was my grandmother's. Around her neck is a string of gold discoloured pearls, and a longer necklace of the coral beads Oshivambo women fasten on their new-borns. It's an outfit in honour of someone who passed away this week. It's soft and quietly elegant. When I sit at my desk, I look out a window that takes up one wall of our flat. It's in an old converted house in a leafy part of London. In the garden, birds are always demanding your attention like the second princess. I've begun to learn their names – Robin, Great Tit, Wren, and Black-tailed Magpie. The fox that has dug itself a den in the garden next door has had pups. There are always sirens and the sounds of construction building up the area to outprice us. There are bluebells and squirrels conducting turf wars. The apiarist next door tends his bees in his white space suit. I love this flat.

I often think I've dreamed it.

Part II

A new view. The same desk. The cat is gone, but there are enough memories of her on the sunshine *stoep* that it feels she could be here, regardless. Around the corner, on an adventure that would have been unthinkable when she arrived to us – a small pile of tortoiseshell fluff, all aquiver.

She hid immediately, the same way I tucked myself in as the third-grade activity to learn fractions, a piece of paper getting smaller, edges less sharp with each fold. What else do you do, when you've packed up a life to catch a flying ship across the sea, only to land in picturesque suburbs of hell?

Then, she crawled back into life – this charity case of a calico cat – with nothing but her capacity to alliterate. Suddenly, there's an adorned mannequin to curl up beneath. It wears a silver sequin dress from a long ago glistening second – opening a car door to pour out, as liquid mercury, to be eyed by the usually cutting housemate who says, 'Leave it to Nica to have to look the best.' Someone feeds her regularly, and says, 'Goodnight, little thing,' each night as she curls up on the couch, below the gleam of fairly lights ordered as a gesture of freedom from the other side of the world.

She saw us through – from that home, into this, surprising all with how she managed packing up a life again to travel to this little house by the bay. She was quiet on the train, although draped in a towel so the noise wasn't quite so saturating. Our little unit, standing beside the tracks, waiting for the friendly she-devil to whoosh us into a future floating beyond the London smog.

On our first day, we retrieved Moomin and her grey spaceship nest, and wandered this new place with them – not yet knowing this wasn't a town to bat an eyelid. It's missing limbs but its hair is long and flowing, and so we were the least of its worries. I saw swans levitating above water and was pulled so hard the truck almost moved me. Then, the salt entered my lungs as alchemy – and I was replete.

So, my desk lounges in a room of its own, and the ghost of the cat sleeps on the new blue futon. We don't usually buy new, and won't again, but to have a piece of furniture all my own in this special, small, room is Virginia Woolf's cream tea.

stoep: porch (Afrikaans)

3

Vallei van Verlatenheid

I have a photograph of a house at sunset
a frontier homestead
with seeping stark dark coffee and
squirmingly luscious white milk

my dad walked me there
he did not want to look inside
he remembers it alive

it's a pirate ship now
alone

he told me to bury him there

I dug a grave
and left him.

Thirteenth

Go slow-ly next time
you are inside of me
I am fragile, a deer
of woven glass. Touch me
as you would plait
a child's hair.

Your fingers are large.
My strings are thin.
And when I am wet,
like paper, I tear.

National University Shutdown, South Africa, October 2015

My lover
there was a day like yours once –
the first of a year, with gin and dry lemon, on a green garden patio,
when I still ate potatoes
how hungry I was
for lif…lov…lear…

I didn't know, then –

Blue dye on voluptuous knees.
A grandmother looks away while a grandson is thrown.
Shopping for nappies for children chased from their homes (and
cigarettes for their mothers).
Thank-full when the priests came – surely they will not hate us
now?
Tearing blackface posters down, trying to breathe through my
breasts.
My voice crawling down my throat to hide in my gut.
Vomiting wheels – my body a small child begging, "Please don't
make me."
"I'm sorry Granny. I can't defend your faith here. They will lynch
me."

Confession

My new friend
was late for her first class
to come to my room
when it was saturated
with dry rice, weeping
and me

She says "It's nice to shout at white people sometimes,"
by way of explanation
as the guys spring with glee
into the melee
with a cyclist (people in Britain shout a lot –
in this only way Westminster excellently represents its constituents.)

Yet,
when she says it
my amygdala clenches

I am 8
hiding my brother
beneath the blankets
both grandmothers made
as my mother kicks
down the lounge door
of pebbled glass
(it shatters as it falls)

I am 10
turning up the animated video
so he cannot hear it
when my father

stands in the street
calls my mother
bitch
from 10 metres away

It's nice to shout at white people sometimes,
she says.

I don't shout at all anymore.

Another Suitcase, Another Hall

It eats me,
through me, you.

It was shoes last time
big black and white Adidas with red rims
I left them at the door,
months after you crossed the border.

I remember my hands shaking
my hand cutting itself
I don't remember anymore
if I fell and you caught me
or you pushed me, and I smashed the coffee cup.

It's juice now
saccharine
forbidden
a glass
calcifying
beside my bed.

Blow-up Doll

My boyfriend's mother
buys me perfume
- it's heavy, strong
a cover-up.

She tells me how nice and thin I am now
- her words, all embedded, 'nice. thin. now.'

She imitates a blowfish
to show me who I used to be
- big and prickly.

His father captures proud photographs
of the day his son carves my big, swollen heart
culled, until it too is nice and thin.

Seashells

I gather seashells like men
make a pretty necklace out of them
mussels
cavalier, cutting, chaotic

I gather seashells with men
wear colour when I write
whelks
timid, taut, territorial

I gather seashells as men
prospect the peaks, touching souls
perlemoen
gleaming, guileless, Godly.

Characters in a Psychologist's Waiting Room

1.   the Girl with eyes wider than her thighs
2.   the Boy who keeps his face covered in the hallways – always
3.   the Woman who sleeps beneath the purple blanket she brings in her bag
4.   there are no men.

Homecoming

I finger through
the plump blush cherries,
pick out the pits, live green stalks

I crunch the chocolate biscuit brownie,
pick the past out of my teeth.

I sip from a black coffee.

I suck the vine leaves' veins,
stain white panties with
beetroot juice.

I twirl spaghetti around fleshy thighs,
grind new boots' heels into gooseberry ghosts
and
mould a child's seashell of an ear
from home-made dough.

(W)him

I am the tooth you tongue
testing the stretch of the ache
an indulgent agony
a flame to finger

but there is another mo(u)th waiting
wet and wanting
to suck the finger
pour neat spirit
bandage the burn
tuck you between breasts
eyes drawn to plump sanctuary
away from me

as I am set alight, again.

Granny Be(a)

I don't know if she called herself an African.
She died before I called myself one.
She died before I called my Self.

She called herself a Catholic.
For her, it meant 'Love thy neighbour'

(not like the white woman who lives next door
strips her boy's ears on Easter Sunday, every Sunday, every day,
until I call Child Protection Services
but doesn't eat meat because it's unethical)

It's raising daughters who skinny-dip, grow hair in their armpits,
ask their Religious Studies teacher how the National Party call
themselves Christians,
eat acronyms UDF-ECC-MDM-TAC-UNESCO in their alphabet
soup.

It's raising sons who tend wounds, save dogs the *boere* make rabid,
shoot their own feet instead of Namibian-Angolan-South
African sons.

They see her in the shape of my mouth.
My mother sees her in my softness.

I tend her
with my crochet
my typing speed
my monogamy
my difficulty losing weight
all a white woman should be when she is born in the 1920s

I tend her
with my humanism
my activism
my writing
my loyalty
my morality
my Spirit
all a white woman is
when she is also an African.

boere: farmer, colloquial term for the police (Afrikaans)

Ewe

When I was 5, my dad left
for work, with long hair, a collar of soft skin.
He came home
choked and shorn
a sheep - led
to Me: the slaughter.

Please

I long for you
to finger my face- lightly
the pad of the fourth on your left hand
to strum my ribs
beneath my breasts that have swollen
to meet terror again,
to gently place your extraordinary eyes on
the spectacle
of
the groaning, lost
organ of me
dragging my weighty, shuddering body
up the African Studies stares
and loving me, privately.

CJR

They say Cecil John Rhodes didn't like women.
He dogs me.

I've known his name longer than I've known it was one.

Before they put the wires in, whenever I close my mouth (often)
my bottom teeth dig small troughs in His gums
my father drives me
on His avenue
to the house
where he left me behind
(he remembers the plants/not his seed)

When I am listening to my history teacher tell me I deserve to be
someone's mother/someone's wife, thinking I should write this
down before I forget I'm worthy
He is ripping my skirt to show my thighs aren't as smooth as my
prose.

After I fled to the closest border town,
tried to love a man who needs a mother and a wife (but not me)
tried to love a cause who needs a writer and a student (but not me)
He claps as the Vice Chancellor calls my name/the dogs.

They have a Dream.

I. They ask if I am excited
and before my fears finish fumbling off my teeth
tell me I am.

They tell me I am going to the oldest university in the world.
I want to say Fatima bint Muhammad Al-Fihriya Al-Qurashiya
founded the University of Al-Karouine in 859.

They tell me an Oxford Masters gets you a job in Holland without
a work visa.
I want to say the leader of the Dutch opposition spews 'the Koran
is fascist.'

I can't talk to my aunts/uncles/cousins/family
friends/neighbours/primary school teachers/shopkeepers/father I
don't talk to anyway/strangers/people I never liked who are proud
of me for living their dream
because they will ask if it is full of wonder
and before the truth seeps out of my mouth
they will tell me it is.

II. I've never seen autumn colours before.
The nights are long, and lovelier for it.
There's a table in a restaurant where women with babies always sit
(different women/different babies).
The women eat bread.
The churches are unlocked.
The boy next door plays piano (loudly) and sings (badly).
The hodgepodge Muslim supermarket reminds me of the corner
cafes where I grew up.
There's a whole society for poetry.

In the pizza place, the chef treats you – as though he has had you over for dinner.

I met an Orthodox priest from Cyprus whose little boy wanted to play with my polka-dot umbrella. I was waiting for a friend – I have friends.

The Provost called me radical.

I told him, "Only in this room."

I walk everywhere. Even at night.

Oxford

Maybe if I ask (smilingly, with a hint of cleavage) for one of them
to beat on me,
they'll work it all out,

their pique that they can no longer chance it
leaving me alive, after
their bemusement that someone will pay for me to learn

Did you know that Her Excellency Doctor Nkosazana Dlamini-
Zuma attained her Bachelors Degree in Science at the University of
Zululand in 1971?
The apartheid state allowed black women to study 14 years before
my College did.

Come to Oxford, the greatest university in the world
(don't worry about forgetting
the architecture/forks/libraries/laundromat will be sure to remind
you)

People/white men like that word nowadays, 'great,'
it smells of empire,
with Eastern Europeans cleaning up the blood, even as it deigns to
spill.

Institutions of Higher Education

I go to university at 18
my dad theorises a 'BA *Mansoek*'
it's an old joke
born decades before me
I cannot expect a man
more Afrikaans than he knows
to be able to say
I am proud
and afraid.

At 21 I am aglow
more educated than any of his line
the BA Man's father & mine talk golf
in a candle-lit living room
my neurons earned
and my bare feet cleaned
the day it is awarded.

At 22 the BA Man
cannot bear the ceremony
it's an old joke
I cannot expect a man
more coward than love
to be able to say
I am proud
and afraid.

I go to Oxford at 25
the burden of all that which I cannot expect
it's an old joke
I am proud and afraid.

Mansoek: seeking a husband (Afrikaans)

You are a Colour

Forgive me my gluttony.
You are a colour.
A pronoun.
A way of being alive.
Forgive me.
I am in the weeds. They are in my mouth.
But this, I can say aloud.

You are glorious.
You will be, always.
This i tell you.
If I am forgotten, downtrodden, disappeared, I will remember you.
You are re-membered, always.

Forgive me.
For loving so fundamentally.
Forgive me.
You are the light, you see, and this ugliness tires me.

Forgive me. For wanting more.
for i believed you
i believed you more
more than the Voice: say nothing, stay still, these are dangerous -
men.

i believed you.
Now you carry the weight when i am afraid and constituted by
death.
Forgive me.
Forgive the truth.
I am never casual.

I am never small.
I am never light.
I am always all.

Forgive me, for believing a boy on his first adventure.
Forgive me my gluttony. I cannot.

Grace

I wish they sold hope
like the sachets of gin in the single store in Kokrobite

I wish promises were like plastic
never broken down.

I wish I knew which wasteland to visit you in.

In my experience,
Grace isn't gracious
it's hard-won
and sworn at God
it's unkempt
and breaking your black streak because the red Alice band is seven
rand cheaper
it's here
when you and I share a room

with all our monsters besides.

Fish

There were weeks spent with my head over the bath,
white girl hair the black baby sucked for the taste of the Exotic
in the small town that stinks of fish – you have to face the sea, or
you can see the gaps where the Germans took the skulls.
My mother picked lice from my head.
I don't know how I caught them – I never left the house.
She ground them dead between ring and thumb fingernails.
Each, a memory of the man who occupied me,
combed out of my temporal lobe
and wiped clean so after, there is only a limpid smell of fish.

Milkbox Tray

I perch in wet grass
sucking chocolates I can't afford
wondering if I will marry
the fiancé at my side

I wedge in wet dirt
lifting the girl
whose sight has just slipped away
telling her help is coming

hoping this sticky world
won't make a liar out of me.

Original Sin

You tell me to forget
the feel of you
around my throat.

There's an AG in NYC
got a law passed
says I was one open mouth (mine)
away from you killing me.

Dylan Farrow's brother wrote another
in Trevor Noah's waiting room
the AG is an Oh no man (here in South Africa we say *Ag nee man*)
throttling, slapping
his mortician's mask slips
as he cums.

Sometimes I believe them
when they tell me
I am paying the price
for my body's sin,
that men are simply ravenous –

Why else are they eating us whole?

Shades of Orange

There was a room in the yellow house, the one my father lived in
after he left us.
It was the colour of James' Giant's Peach's guts.
It was the only room in the house with a lock.
I knew of a boy whose teachers beat him pre-emptively,
a Monday morning ritual.
I, as a child whose voice-box was charged pre-emptively with
dissent,
sat in that room watching the tap drip when called for dinner on
white lace.
But Dad, I remember when you lived with us.
Dad, Mom is drinking.
Dad, I was late for school yesterday for the weeping.
Dad, the students' eyes were unknowably wide as I shuffled in.
Dad, this woman you call your wife came to our home for band practice. My
mother made her tea. She wore a mauve beret, and I thought her chic with
youth.
Dad, this leaping dog frightens me. When it leaps to greet me, it may jar loose
my tongue.
Dad, why do you already hate me for what I could say?

I sat watching the tap trip into the sink
and thought to myself, anywhere else I'd twist it hard
seal its wound.
But here, in this house of fragrant white lace,
I sit in the room of lurid peach guts,
watching the water run.
Red-eyed and silent, I think
in this one way, I will cost you.

October's Birmingham

In Birmingham, I am in proportion.
My white made less off with the wide culture wheel.

The bachelorette's peach underwear my cousin buys three months
early
(flights are *duur* & home's displacement long)
hold my hips as hands.

The French café presents a platter of madeleines.
I see a tray of small girls,
blonde and booted for drizzling Paris, and
somewhere I have a sister.

We walk within the Bog they say inspired JR's Dark Forest.
My feet ache only somewhat
as my in law talks the Angolan headlands
and I am the green of trees in the shade before autumn.

I tell a new friend I love him for the first time.
I've lived here four years.
It took that time for my mouth to recall how to sing.
Love must be sung.

*duur: expensive (Afrikaans)

Disability Advice

Do you know what isn't in the pamphlets the kind, inert Disability
Advisory Service woman offers,
when you have panic attacks as regularly
as most slug coffee
in this secretly bruising student town?

How do you not cut your self
shaving
or carry un-shattered dishes
to the sink?

Speaking of control,
how do you press
Ctrl S?

There is no consent to be asked when limbs earthquake.

I walked home alone today.

One walk
One tranquiliser
One break
But I made it
Then I shaved.

Virus 2.0

It slips past in a Natural Science classroom when you are 14.
It is familiar already- the second cousin who brings an open bottle
of vodka to family occasions.
But now it is the sentence subject.
Your diligent right hand notes it legibly in blue.
Ah, but your left.
Your left palm has a drummer boy's fingers prancing upon it.
So, you miss it that first time.
That word – virus
Which pins you in the city of your grandmother's comedies
Young, newly wed, alive
Afraid.

Part II
They say it's like drowning
You think, 'That's alright, then.'
You remember sinking in a foreign feudal town
When you took your body swimming in pinched nylon
To try to remind your lungs how to move.

You thought you'd need a swimming cap
They laughed
Silly child
Here, someone is paid to pick hairs from the anchor's chain.

The Lancing

Let us drink water together.

Let's walk on the clean fine sand
where we have wept
spun webs of wishing.

There is pain in the glass
like a spirit, it burns

We froth with trembling
I am a'feared
But the love is lanced
And runs clean.

Modern Medicine

In Lesser Evils
a doctor's alibi
is his indifference –
his favourite patient is unconscious
(a skill I lack).

The nurse whistles through her teeth,
tells me to stop eating
when I tell her my weight
(I've just left the psych ward,
not for my recalcitrant eating disorder.)

The anaesthetist doesn't read any of the 8 forms,
is surprised to discover I take Schedule 5 drugs while wheeling me
to surgery.
(He casually recommends Electric Shock Therapy,
is entertained when my bleeding mouth asks if the screaming
woman is alright.)

He reassures me –
he also went to my university
the one named for an imperialist.
(He sighs those were the good old days.)

I am ashamed I do not tell him he is wrong.
I am afraid.
I am a psych patient, naked under my hospital gown.

He wants to run electricity into my brain -
what will he do if I tell him which side of the barricades I stood on?

How

No-one taught me how
to do the loving

Father hugged Mother from behind once -
it made me feel peculiar -
why was he touching her?

Aunts married boys
Uncles married wives

Mother and Grandmother are women alone.

In the news, women are paragons or corpses.

"He's a keeper," Mother says

How-
how do I keep two people alive?

First Friend

We eat artichokes with our knees
touching
they were my first solid.
my dad raised them
outside my window
dipped in gold glass
for me to swallow.

I dig the flesh out
with my tight two top teeth
(no passion gap in ye olde England)

I eat them illicitly now
at a small mosaic table
with eyes alight.

We swap stories and skins
here, where I take care -
to place unpedicured toes between cracked cobblestones.
Step on a crack, little girl, sin
little girl, stumble into hell.

Here,
there's a single coat
on the back of my chair.

it isn't mine –
how sublime.

An Oshivambo Patsy Cline

When my Ma starts drinking again,
I try to be her friend,
instead of my fear.
I play Patsy's *She's Got You Babe*
tell her how 'I got your picture, but she got you babe,'
makes me think of her and the empty frames and full bottles my
father left behind.

She leaves the room.

I wear his beads,
the pink coral fingernail cuttings
that his Me tells me she placed around his neck
after birthing him
as we sit on her bed
that speaks of my *Ouma*
and she gifts them to me -
a noose.

I listen to Beth Hart's *Tell Her You Belong to Me*
& wonder, absently,
where will his new lover get her beads?

*Ouma: Grandmother (Afrikaans)

Thirst

I lived in a land of drought
stark, harsh
do not smuggle your stepmother's shampoo
her hair is lush with water
and your father's love
her skin – never scrubbed
she grows roses
pretty, greedy and foreign
you are small, untidy, tough
a *boer*
you belong to broken lands like this one.

boer: farmer/Afrikaner (Afrikaans)

Like Riding a Bike

I rode my bicycle to buy a pregnancy test
made sure to tell the cashier that's why I was sweating
she wore diamantes in her ears
my friend's mother saw me
adult,
all wrapped-up in her wedding rings and boastful menopause.
My favourite polka-dot shorts felt sinful
suddenly —
they show too much thigh
are the type worn by a little girl.
There's no dignity to it
despite the layers of foil/contained cap.
I told the cat to leave me alone.
This was private.

Accra

I could tell you how, despite all my efforts with conservative dress, the front breast button on my shirt kept popping open during my induction.

I could tell you of the difficulty of dental hygiene when mouth-friendly water comes in packets.

I could tell you of being hissed at by a man in the street.

I could tell you of prayer camps where mentally ill people are taken to be purified.

I could tell you of watching one young boy furiously stir, as another fervently fans off the flies.

I could tell you of a little girl who lives in an orphanage because she was cast out as a witch.

I could tell you of constantly being pestered by men.

I could tell you of the school I saw which lacks teachers because those the government sends take one look at the basic conditions, leave to "fetch their things," and don't come back again.

I could you tell you of being called to fetch my order — "Obruni!" (meaning "White!")

I could tell you of stepping out my door, and knowing that everyone who sees me knows I do not belong.

I could. But...

I can tell you of the pleasure of hearing Agnes, who made my order, call "Nica!" for the first time. I can tell you of the sweet, warm taste of grilled plantain, the relief when a bucket of water finally cascades down over you, and the sight of a woman lifting the basket to balance on the material donut on her friend's head. I can tell you of such a basket, lined with live chickens clucking away on their unusual perch, a baby black goat strolling the street like an Enid Blyton nursery rhyme, the sublime justice of sweet and sour pineapple hacked up and tossed in a plastic bag for serving, and the strain of music that clips in through the window of the *tro* making my surroundings a film.

I can tell you of the canoe pilot who made each girl a necklace from a waterlily he plucked from the Amansuri wetland. I can tell you of a teacher who speaks of Project Citizen, Rights & Responsibilities Day, and the Freedom Fighters choir at his high school.

I can tell you of the dresses, and the wry experience of seeing such an elegant woman spit. I can tell you of listening to Ghanaian rap in an internet café with an orange *stoep*, alone with two unknown men at night — the most foreign experience so far.

tro: Ghanaian minibus taxi
stoep: porch (Afrikaans)

First Daughter

There was always one dark room in the house.
On a desk carved out of an old packing crate, proclaiming FRAGILE, squatted a computer, porcelain fairies missing hands-ears-heads, a red chess timer, and an old *mielie*. It moved with the packing crate desk, house to house, wife to wife. A new wife calling for dinner. A new family left waiting. A new blonde-ringleted daughter delivering tea to go undrunk, and fairies to go unfixed.
It shed jewels of corn until it was nothing but that for which the word 'husk' was formed. Still it stayed.
Midst painfully vast fields of harvest, an aching sight in a country so hungry, an out-of-place *boer* hands her a mielie. His *kortbroeke* are too short, he is gross with sweat, but he performs the traditional national greeting — three kisses — with endearing eagerness.
The *mielie* is slid into the First Daughter's hand perfunctorily. She grips it greedily.
When no-one is looking she will place it in her bag. She will fight the Congolese Customs agent who eventually just chuckles at white girl silliness.
She will place it on her desk — where there are no broken fairies, in a room that is not dark.
It, she, is not a husk.

*mielie: corncob (Afrikaans)
*boer: farmer/Afrikaner (Afrikaans)
*kortbroeke: short pants (Afrikaans)

Staying Alive

It's a disease of disappearance. When sewing a hole closed, you select thread that will curate seamlessness. With this disease of stolen Memory, you want thick orange thread, sewn in a distinct hand. At least then you know something is missing. It begins with the memory of Joy, but it is thorough. You forget how coffee tastes — and then how to taste it, even when it is in your mouth. You forget not to put metal in the microwave, and then when it is exploding, you forget why. You forget how to move your arm, to stir sugar in, to shove away the man in the mask.

That's why they put you in the same ward as the old folks, the ones who need watching — those who might place a spoonful of leaky scrambled eggs in their mouths and then forget how to chew. And instead, choke.

I kept being put in baths.

When I was eight, we went on a family holiday to the Cedarberg. It rained — eighty mm of melted snow filled the floor of the empty dam. My big cousin and I ran through one of those sharp winter mornings when it hurts to breathe but it burns lovingly to laugh. We climbed into the dam to escape the pack of sheepdog puppies. We named their leader Zeus.

We dared each other: kneel in the water. Sit in it. Lie down.
We arrived home two stuttering ice cubes, stinging with the thrill of getting all our warm clothes wet. My mom stripped us, forcing us into a luke-warm bath where we sat, a gaggle of tingling goose-pimpled limbs, giggling at our brilliant audacity.

Fifteen years later this memory is gone — the hole stitched seamlessly closed — as I am forced into a bath. This time, loose-limbed with Valium, the ice doesn't melt.

Hospitalized. My world shrinks to my ward — and the coffee shop downstairs, which serves spicy sausages and sweet potato slap tjips. I am woken by a nurse who is supposed to take my vitals — blood pressure, temperature, pulse. Sometimes he makes them up. But he always smiles nicely, a defiant act in a psychiatric ward at six thirty A.M.

There's a kind of status to it when your doctor comes. It takes precedence. They'll wake you if you're asleep, your breyani will congeal beneath its cling-wrap, your gobs of acrylic paint will dry in the Occupational Therapy room. The nurse says, "Your doctor is here," and you shuffle your slippers extra loud as you go down the corridor towards the locked ward door.

It's a cold room — a couch, a desk, the window that looks out at nothing. And a small stadium of a clock. The psychiatrist never has long. A small plastic cup is placed in your hand on your way back to your bed. The nurse has to see you swallow. The anti-depressant is red. The anti-anxiety white. The tranquiliser blue. A European flag-ful of colours.

Pills are somehow scarier in an unmarked plastic cup. They could be anything, do anything. Lap you in nausea. Or heat that doesn't register on a thermometer but makes you pointedly pretty with flush, except for the sweat.

At two A.M., your body is dunked in adrenalin as the sleeping pills wear off. It's the witching hour described by the little girl in Roald

46

Dahl's *Big Friendly Giant* — awake at an orphanage at midnight, no body allowed out of bed.

You're hungry sometimes. Never at mealtimes. The friendly kitchen lady encourages you to rush to lunch or Doreen makes balloons of the plastic sheeting that covers the unripe fruit. No-one begrudges her the fun but when she pops them everyone's anxiety gets triggered. Or PTSD.

You accumulate hours outside. Except for the smokers who venture onto the balcony enclosed by blunted glass. I've always been fixated with balconies. This one feels like a prison yard, with a discarded treadmill picking up rust and nicotine.

But, at least, you can see **up**.

One of the few moments of family unity that I recall took place in a bathroom, too. There was a bath, a basin, a toilet, and a window through which you could examine people's feet. There's a parent in the bath, a whole family in that little room.

I am being told happy news. A brother is coming. There is delight. Later…after the baby is born, the mother hospitalised, the father absconded…I hide in the bathroom in his new house.

It has a lock on the door and it's taboo to bother a person in the bathroom (they could be shitting).

So I sit on the edge of the goddamned house and watch the water drip into the bath.

In any other place, I move to close the tap.
In any other place, I can move.

47

A Political Country

On Friday, my father tells me not to talk Politics.
On Saturday, he assures his expat South African friends that his
daughter's activism
      saturates him with hope.
On Sunday, he shows me the desolate family farm.
On Monday, a national shutdown begins.
On Tuesday, a man pulls a gun at a barricade while I'm ladling
sunscreen.
On Wednesday, a national march strolls the rich side of town.
On Thursday, we open a barricade for an ambulance of
suicide/vans of evacuees.
On Friday, my boyfriend hides in my house because he is
Namibian.
There are men with cricket bats at the doughnut counter. But don't
talk politics here.

Humanity

Genitalia are not good-looking.
Don't get me wrong – I love my man's manhood, and my
womanhood.
Although those particular terms fit like a T-shirt I wore when I was
eight.
Tight and too starched.
I cut my nails too short on a lot of words
but is that what my womanhood looks like?
Pink origami mountains.
Or my man's manhood
A crayon that's been smudged round.
I wish I could paint his toenails green
instead of his painting
my eyelids blue.
But that's humanity,
a belly flop on the pool of life,
and as a feminist
that's my policy.
I think I've chosen delta
as the title
for the folds between my legs
that are something ancient and symbolic
and still fairly weird
and not particularly pretty.
Genitalia aren't good-looking
but humanity is gorgeous.

Written & Performed in Ukuphuthelwa (Insomnia)

As I lay on a boy's floor
and inhaled his dust
which became the earth of a father's grave,

he gave me water to wet my tongue
which became rain
that made mud of the earth,
spattering shit-chills on my chicken-skin calves.

I tasted the air of his bedroom
which became the brunt
of the reader's red wine.

The scrape of the rug on my blush-blessed cheek
became the blackening burn
of my cigarette's throat.

I tipped the ash
as I hear the coffin's shrug – into the *gat*
of the earth.

*gat: hole (Afrikaans)

Autobiography

In 93, in-heat, I was borne, of two days' labour
for a mother eating chocolate-dunked ice-cream
also bearing arrows dipped in blue.
Else-Where, a long-haired father played his Castle in a half-
kamer, waiting news - his annual actions had borne fruit.
Mother and Lump crossed – I gave him my first smile.
He never paid me back.
98, I 100-pieced puzzles, checksing Disney at a friend.
She died. 'They' gave me her Barbies instead.
It wasn't enough.
I tattooed a reminder on - (Loved Ones Leave).
99, television: I dreamed a TwisterPro could
kru-krux-crash World-Wide-Wrongs like peanuts.
Millennium Came, orgasmed in the sky... I inked my lessons in:
people cheer louder when terrified.
2000's: Bro: born. Mother: exhausted. Father: left.
I said my first Fuck, began to eat white bread.
Granny remixed my faith, with As Time Goes By and YOU.
She died in 05.
I killed myself
on stage,
for the first but not last time.
December 06: let cane lash my spine, crackling roast my belly,
wine soil itself on my tongue.
07, A lovely boy linked himself to me, saying I love you
in spite of the dirt.
I said it back, hid mine in the shade of his neck.
WRITTEN: first novel manuscript Marriage2Death (70 000
words).
I wore my bought-for-First-Date-and-backed-out-of-wearing-Red-
Dress to celebrate "The End."

I divorced that life, happy *om his hand te hé*.
I scratched at my tattoo. It murmured back.
I said Goodbye to his safe-shade: on the phone, *nogal*.
One Cowardly Act that determined the necessity of
future bravery.
So I left. St(reet)-rode out, beyond the known horizon.
09, I stepped on stage, unclamped my tonsils, sang.
I found a church in which to weep, and I was safe as no-one
spoke my *taal*;
God sat beside me.
And we held each other's hands.

10, I perched on the Matric Fountain rim, a gift of a previous
time, and hack-coughed up chunks of my hurted heart.
Died on stage again, burning house & audience down.
An earring for an A. Total 6 shot into my lobes in One Day.

A Father of Four said: You deserve to be someone's Mother,
Someone's Wife. 8 words to save a life.
11, *Oom* believed me when I told my dad-story.
I took a friend to Temple on the day of Rebirth:
ate: Lindt
slept: late
read: The Secret Magdalene
shared: faith
I put on a fat suit and sang:
YOU CAN'T STOP MY HAPPINESS BECAUSE I LIKE THE
WAY I AM.
In the a.m., I learned Human Rights practice as a volunteer.
In the p.m., I taught it to students at Accra High.
Whilst there, I swallowed, sweated out my Fear.
12, I chose an institution.
The VC said it chose me too –

we both submit stretch marks, evidence.
I
approachbluffconsiderdesireexpressforgetgrappleharmonize
idealize*jol*knowlearnmanagenitpickoscillatepreconceivequietreco
nfigurestruggletranscribeunderstandvacillatewonder...
ex-traordinary and exasperating: the question of Why?

*kamer: room (Afrikaans)
*om his hand te hé: to have his hand (Afrikaans)
*nogal: moreover (Afrikaans)
*taal: language (Afrikaans)
*Oom: Uncle (Afrikaans)
*jol: party (Afrikaans

Desdemona's Toothbrush

Nobody is impressed by implicits.
Star-crossed lovers make for dull dinner guests,
and Rapunzel's sun-golden string still splits.
And each newlywed separately rests
in-between sex, and shits out foreign dessert.
On proposal, daddy issues don't ditch.
Austen died young, Shakespeare cheated – an expert?
On expiring life, the romantic's itch.
NB Query: would you change history?
Makers of Darcy & Desdemona
making grammar and vocabulary…
Or leaver of toothpaste, lease co-owner?
Had it happened, there's no sonnet to mock.
We'd be at the mercy of Doctor Spock.

Pandora

During the dying of the decade,
there is shrieking jubilation

I reserve my quiet
beneath the floorboards
of my husband's wife's home

Hoping
if I hide until the clocks change
it remains unseen
if
I slip the box.

Travelling with Kapuscinski

The first place I read Kapuscinski's *Travelling with Herodotus* was the hospital at the foot of the mountain. He describes becoming infatuated with the idea of crossing a border, any border. Where everyone sees snakes, he sees ladders. I am walking a ward: psychiatrist's office, nurse's station, bed with blue curtain, bathroom with flooded floor, Occupational Therapy room which catches the sun as it sets. My mind is in hiding. When they take me to the park, the colours scald my neurons. But I can read. For the first time in months, maybe years. I can read for the brunch of it. I read Kapuscinski decades before, as he reads Herodotus centuries before that.

I have read him before, on another bed, in a tiny town heaving with history. Where I come home from my first African Studies lesson abashed by how many countries I left unnamed in the introductory quiz that shamed us all. Or should have, anyway. I write them out in black permanent marker on thin white paper, puttied to the cobbled, bleached lemon walls. I read him on the Soviet Union as it breaks apart like icebergs on a Warm War. He seduces me pinned in a tiny loud plane – and then frightens me in a silenced speck of a town. I give the book away for fear of looking too close at the silent world cracked open. It's contagious, you know, the end of silences. I still need mine.

I read him again in a queue in the desert, as I wait to climb the (hu)man-made structure they've built to set alight. I hear the silence of noon in the Somalian desert on the walk from Berbera to Laascaanood – and the ballad, "My country? My country is where the rain falls," as I stand apart at an occasion with the hubris to name itself 'Africa Burns.' She does – and there are no medics on standby.

56

I am grateful for the medic when he finds me on my hands and knees, glasses broken, with the pulsing blood pudding spilling from my mouth, a cup of bitter *boere koffee* churning with the sand of a different desert or two.

I sit chuckling at the absurdity of holding the book with bandaged hands and learning through a broken lens about a coup in Liberia – Kapuscinski sees the film of Prince Johnson's torture of Liberian leader Samuel Doe in a bar. I see the richest of the people playing at poor take off at the airstrip. I am pleasantly surprised to find I can once again laugh.

I read him on my carefully timed lunchbreaks from selling my soul – typing captions and metadata for paparazzi agencies in other countries. I learn that *Love Island*, Tommy Robinson, Lisa Curry, and Winter Wonderland exist.

I find a stack of his books in the first ever Oxfam bookshop. It's a small, warm, and empty store. I use scholarship money to buy them. I don't look at the prices which I find novel and glorious. He writes about borders – turning them over on his tongue, letting them fizz like sherbet in a small secret packet. Customs is an apt moniker, for those who guard the gates, and dictate where a state begins. In Kinshasa, they wonder aloud which of my parents is African because of my curvy flesh. It could only be one, they're sure, because the white skin has to come from somewhere else. In the no-man's-land between Ghana and Togo, he asks why I am wearing a wedding ring. When I explain it staves off men (who only see my exotic body), he offers to marry me with my passport under his thumb. In Tankwa Town, two lithe naked white people throw sand over you and laugh. In London, they are jovial. They can afford to be. They already have my English test and lung scan for TB on file.

I've lived here two years now, married to a citizen of the as yet still United Kingdom for one. My visa has floated for a year and a third, 16 months, 500 days...my body, African white it is, requiring three psychotropic drugs on a good day, could create and birth a new life in less time than it takes the "WORLD-BEATING SYSTEM" to decide how far into our home the South African border comes.

No family member stood by me at my civil ceremony. My brother did not walk me down the aisle (they did not believe his South African university education was sufficient proof he would leave again). My sister has gone from child to teenager unheld by me. My best friends have left a space where their bridesmaid would be.

I cannot leave while they debate my future. But I am travelling again. I am in Uzbekistan with Colin Thubron; on the Mediterranean with David Abulafia; in Cairo with Amitav Ghosh; with Kapuscinski at the foot of the mountain.

boere koffee: Afrikaans coffee

What's That?

The student says, "What's that?" He is a friend, and not cruel by nature, although prone to discomforting bouts of speech. He informs me that that my first time having sex will be a public performance. He is gangly and wears too short yellow shorts when not performing, when he has some magic to ooze cool. Enough to make him golden at our high school and a pop star later. But now he is the young man pointing at my vagina, in a circle of our teenage friends, asking, "What's that?"

The shame is excruciating.

He is still the only person I've ever offered to invest in, in that brief moment when I earn significant money. I cannot comprehend his question. I am wearing royal purple leggings and he is 18. There is somehow too much curl to the convex, too much flesh to a part of me barely touched by anyone (including myself). I reply with boldness borne of shame's spotlight, "My vagina." The group laugh a shuffling laugh of awkwardness and move on. I never forget. I ask my husband years later if my vagina is, in that eternal of girl's fears, too fat. I cannot force it to fold more of itself in.

I loved him, a touch. Attended his first solo show at a casino on my own. Wrote to him years later when he participated in a foolish magazine shoot in a women's magazine, marking the ever strangely commemorated South African Women's Month by putting well known men (including a known abuser) in heels so they could reflect on the difficulties of being a woman. I thought I had a duty to gently explain why people were seething. He never replied.

He found me compelling once. We loved each other gently. But he's the boy who asked, "What's that?" marking out my vagina as wrong, somehow too much in the world.

The dentist says, "Open wide," & the giggles I'm holding in my oesophagus almost escape. It's the morning after the first time.

There is such hope to sex then. We waited a year; washed each other's nakedness in bucket showers when the running water decides it doesn't run in our town again. Students protest against the lacklustre municipality – one girl we know wears just a towel in the Hellenic colours. But we are sealed in the boys' bathroom in his university dormitory named for Voortrekker Piet Retief, where we close eyes in glee and tip the buckets over each other. We are practiced – he, from visits to the North of Namibia to see family, and I, from living in Accra, Ghana, as a human rights volunteer. We've done this and more for each other, long before sex quietly approached us. Lust takes many forms.

His mother didn't let us share a bed at his shadowed home in Windhoek, with the home's embroidered testimonials of Christ. I didn't understand then that it was kept dark to keep the glistening heat out. All I could think was how it echoed my *Ouma's* curtained home in the Klein Karoo, crocheted toilet seats and all. My Ouma who, were I to bring him to her, would not embrace this tall young black man. But his mother's aesthetic mirrors her, my Afrikaans *Ouma*. His mother welcomes me with the precious pink Oshivambo coral beads and a vivid pink ballooning dress.

His mother didn't let us share a bed while mine dropped us at the bottom of the hospital's hill for my intra-uterine device. We walked up in a cloud, sluggish with thought. This was not young romance, but it also was, taking care of my body together. My government would pay for me to open my legs and have a metal trickery device slid inside. We made it to the top of the hill, but the correct nurse wasn't in. So we left the place where they first took a young girl's heart and placed it in a man's chest – where it beat for 18 days of miracle.

He was a'fear that day, & couldn't face it again the next. I don't know why. I should have asked. I was preoccupied, keeping my facial muscles still, compacting my secret woman's rage. It was, after all, me who had to lie on the bed and open wide.

So, I paid the only doctor in our far-flung town to do it months later. He wore safari shorts, *kortbroeke nogal*, and had framed photographs of his two tooth-gapped daughters lying on a rug – the skin of some animal he'd shot. Again, we sat throbbing silently in a waiting room. Again, I insisted he join me and he did (I insisted on even less then.) It was my warmth that was set to be invaded – again, he was a'fear. There was a reason. There must have been. He was always protective. His mother raised him to walk on the side of the road, and carry all my groceries.

But I couldn't think about that, while towering safari suit man told me, "Sometimes we have to stop – if you pass out from the pain." He'd forgotten the scissors to cut the strings, so he left me leaking blood, almost glibly, onto the plastic hospital bed and – leaving the consultation room door open – went hunting again.

After, when I sat in the chair in the room with the dead animal pictures, he told me earnestly that I could still "service my boyfriend," while we waited for my womb to issue an official reply to this latest development. I almost giggled for the shock of it. Was this happening? These two absurd men, floating bubbles of fear &

61

smugness that passed through the wall to the waiting room, engaging in a secret pact over my womb.

The writer said nothing as his foot nudged between my legs again, again. We just watched each other and whispered across the smoothed chlorinated water. He is floating in a lime green plastic donut. I am standing in the shallow end, bobbing in years' of unnamed desire, as I use the waves to bring the uncrisped donut to me gently again, again.

The body sits beneath me, dripping loathing on the floor as toffee. It is all in the glare, caught in a farmhouse of mirrors, *boere bene* prickled with hair, fleshy arms with dead pixels of skin, a smashed pout above sweating chin crease and beneath a veld of tiny hairs. It, not she, folds in half at a white desk tip-tip-typing away, back to the *koppie* pleading for reprieve.

*_kortbroeke nogal:_ shorts, moreover (Afrikaans)
*_boere bene:_ farmer/Afrikaner legs (Afrikaans)
*_koppie:_ hill (Afrikaans)

A Cheap Pink Ring Box

Where does the love go when it is over?
I'm not sure I'll ever be able to wholly explain any of it.
How to shape my teeth around the words that a man I loved (with
embarrassing thoroughness as I did all things) bought me a thin silver
ring on the final day - that the woman behind the counter recognised
him and I together as the unit we'd once been ... when buying foolish
toys and trinkets for birthdays and anniversaries stretched out across
four years like a gradually chafing skipping rope.

He insisted – that I select which piece of metal I'd remember him
by, only hours after he twisted his long, elegant fingers around that
final nylon string linking our fates; closed short, twirling eyelashes;
and pulled. On-stage, only meters from where he first found and
loved you, a quiet tugging began that has yet to cease, six wide years
and an ocean later.

The stage leans in a building they call a living monument to the poor,
white, tough lives fleeing a war-ravaged Britain to form a human
frontier against the amaXhosa in their own homeland. Samuel and
Harriet were born in London, a city I'd arrive in 237 years later, and
brought here on a ship named for the Greek goddess of the dawn.
After 90 days at sea, they stepped into this country of mine – where
they would join the dust of this town where I, their descendant,
would love this tall, tense man.

I chose simply. A silver ring, an almost wedding band, to wrap the
last coils around. And because he urged me to with ragged eyes - I
retrieved a small pink ring box with plastic gold mouldings from his
calcite palm. It is cheap and soft to touch, as I felt with four years of
my soul seeping through his unclenched hands. My palm cuts itself
that day, while seated at the café waiting for him to arrive to quietly

negotiate the logistics of my loss. The barista greeted me with joy and asks after my lover by name. He too remembers us as two.

What do I say to these signposts, this tour of remembered quiet loving, as they smile gleefully at me from what is - as of only minutes ago - my past? My eyes are wearing contact lenses, my body draped in my graduation gown. How do I say, he arrived from across the border with minutes to spare ... and skipped it? A terrible verb, latent with casual-ty. How do I admit what is abruptly true? It wasn't enough. I loved him. He loved me. It wasn't enough.

He has arrived in the town where we kept each other alive through the xenophobia/He knows you won't attack him, though; misogyny/I know who you are. You're his bitch; racism/He pulls you closer to deepen the crusty white woman's frown at our entwined hands.

There were clusters of soft, living things midst the haze of being taught to want less of life. For the world was devastatingly cruel. And we were not. But we used up our magic in getting out alive and together. We, neither, were what some South Africans wanted to see: me on a barricade and him in hiding.

The e-tv talk shows are correct. Boundaries and communication are vital − but no one spoke of how to do that in a place with threat congealing as smog. What is the "proper degree of terror," Lord Graham, for whom the town where we fell into love was named, administered on the amaXhosa? Administered, as if colonisation belongs to the world of paper cuts. They've changed the name now, and rightly so. My movement would have rejoiced then. Some would dance on tables in Council Chambers and ululate. But when I speak of that time, the tongue that did not yet know wholly how to love a man's body ensnares itself *oppad na die pleknaam toe*. My body still knows it lived in Graham's Town.

Still, we met. I was worried I'd failed my first Philosophy test. He was beautiful, and I was made brave by drink. I took his hand, and startlingly, we're kissing in a room of sweat, shards of light, and spirit. I am unlike my scared self and it is sublime. He insists on walking me home, but I won't leave the hideout of smoky gloom where he has spent hours marking my neck with his patient, square teeth. I know tomorrow there will be fear again. So, it is in the final hours of dark when we sit on the ugly green bench outside the Philosophy department. I want to kiss him there in a young girl's notion of defiance: say I am more than my mind – I am also the body this man is lusting.

My university has still not changed its white supremacist name, but I've been stumbling on that one for years. I applied to the university furthest away from my town. I've always been thus – both bold and terrified. My acceptance letter was sent to Accra, where my Ghanaian supervisor Ebenezer at the human rights office convinces me: you'll be able to do more of this work and be better at it. My orientation booklet didn't forewarn, but I should have paid more attention on those Scripture Union camps I attended so as not to be left out. In Samuel 4:1, Eben-Ezer is a battleground.

In a year of protests, he joined me once. It is the day of the national march for equitable access to higher education. There are many more than usual, and more than the usual handful who look like me. Representatives of the movement of which I am a member tell white students to form a buffer, in case the police decide today is the day. I am one of the few who moves. He only joins later, running from class – when all the new faces have collectively refused. I am relieved he was not there to see them part us. He is nervous anyway, always aware of his status as a foreigner in my land. I don't tell him, but I try to place my small, soft lighter body between his larger, leaner, darker one and the edge of the crowd. I feel foolish and unsure as I do. He would be righteous with rage if he knew. He doesn't like me to be on the roadside of pavements, even on the ordinary days that once were – us strolling hand-in-hand on these same streets. We're headed home with grapes, bread and cheese, to picnic on his narrow single bed in his residence named for Voortrekker Piet Retief or in mine, named for anti-apartheid activist Victoria Mxenge (most students call it The Vic to avoid the click). If I wasn't so tired, I'd gaze at the ghosts of those two who viewed their racial, national, and class differences as almost idiosyncratic. We were so different yet found nothing but grace in the touch of each other's skin. Sometimes naivete is necessary.

But that day, I'm too far for even the ghosts to reach. I'm relieved he is visiting my world – and praying no-one gets hurt. Still, even here, as he found me in the crowd, walking beside him makes a flapping vine shyly curl itself back around my spine. It's a little too tight, but still, I am upright again. My prayers are futile, of course. It is the violence I did not yet conceive that has been birthed this day. A different, even more desperate thread in Graham's Town has snapped. A taxi driver protest comes undone midst horror. The whispers following the discovery of a young woman's body parts in a freezer have combusted. In fear, frustration, resentment, and the hopelessness of 70% unemployment, the looting of spaza shops owned by foreigners unspools. Police, who were warned what was burbling and refused to clarify the case, simply stake out a barrier between the two sides of town. It is our Town vs Gown, and I am on a barricade again, when the message comes that the university is evacuating foreign students onto campus. He doesn't go. He sees his friends settled then hides in my home. I am thus not with comrades when the news comes that we have won a victory, small as it is. Fees

DICTION

Words
When birthed by
The forced union
Between violent vowels
And raped consonants
Exhibit a temper unmanageable
They kick
Fine tuned phrases
Into senseless gibberish
Leaving them sore
And paralyzed
And strung into weeping
Limping sentences
That will at once
Dazzle and befuddle...
Till a connoisseur with
Archimedean ecstasy
Emerges naked from
A dip in encyclopedic waters
Grasping a choked verse
Which gasps astounded
Like a beached mermaid.
Stunned and undeafeaned
To its captor's shout of
"Eureka!!"

EMPTY TALK

I have had conversations
With empty beer bottles
I have listened quietly
To tear wrenching tales
From these hitherto carriers
Of a potency distilled to pose
As wit and wisdom

They told me
Father drank his all
One queer day
When the sun rose
From the west
Sending birds into
Confused slumber,

And with much the same aplomb
Without shame or remorse
The contents of the bottles
slew father

FORLORN

Sometimes loneliness
Has enticing appeal
It courts you with
Dusty visage
Punctuated by
A gap-toothed smile
Triggered by none
Other activity
But the sight of you
Seated upon your dreams
In this forlorn corner
Of God's creation
Where barrenness is
The way of life
Even in the face of
Fertile reflections
Garnered from a world-weary soul
Whose feet have chosen
Their own itinerary
And led one to perch
On the seat of a silence
Loaded with whisperings
Of ancient and endless gods
Whose remains remain buried
Under the scorching earth
But whose spirit
Will eternally roam in reign
In this land of grotesque grandeur

SUSPICION

What if the cows
Do not come home
What if they are
Also missing from the pasture?
Will that peaceable crocodile
Who has lived all his life
In still waters
Where the herd drank
And sated mammoth thirsts
Without losing any of their number:
Will such crocodile
Who has suppressed
Natural inclinations
To feed on mud like catfish
Will he be looked at
With same regard and tolerance,
When the cows do not come home
And there's silence
In the kraals?

NOMADS

Today I shall pass by
That intersection once more
Where cars ferrying travellers
Of fate and chance converge
Some driving into unknown lands
To seek the destiny of their imaginations
And others following like accidental disciples
in fervent pursuit
Fleeing their own demons

I shall look away again today
When the one-legged beggar
Propped up on expensive crutches
Extends a well-fed arm
Seeking alms
Under the unaffected witness
Of glass-eyed traffic lights
That glare and stare
And wink authoritatively
With reddened eyes
And for a transient moment
Coalesce nomadic strangers
To outstare each other
with rude wonderment
As they pause from
treading tedious roads
that lead to nowhere

DAYS THAT MATTER

The days that matter
Are not these
That sit stagnant
On the calendar
Staring endlessly at eternity
Whilst the throat of time
Has vomited them
Into the pit toilet
Where clean futures
Frequent to spew
Diarrheal discharges
Into the path of hope
Days that matter
Are yet to be born
These I see in my dreams
Days not strung together
In seconds and minutes
On the strings of patience
Like the waist beads
Of a pagan temptress
Enticing and mysterious
And open to exploration
By any who would
Muster courage
To stare and wink

WET DREAMS

He stood in the rains
As wet dreams
Fell with shameless abandon
From the heavens
He stood without umbrella
Soaking to the bone
But somewhere at his centre
A fire burnt persistently
And refused to be doused
He felt a heat colonise him
And his body responded
Tinglingly with pleasure-pain
He wanted to scream
He wanted to dance
He wanted to laugh,
But still he remained rooted
Married to the muddy reality
And the slippery hope
That impossible it was
To successfully navigate
And so he lingered there
Lifting his face to the skies
Seeking to glimpse the face of She
Who always came faithfully
As drizzle of healing rain
During times of drought
When seeded affection
Lay burning and dying
In girls' rocky hearts

SELF POTRAIT

im here
but you can't see me now
look
im cunningly disguised
like the smell within the fart
invisible but pervasive
occupying the space
that you flee
like the suppressed orgasmic scream
in the grab and toss confusion
of rapist-victim encounter

im here
a wordcrook
verbal ninja
slicing your thoughts
with deformed metaphor and form
twisting and turning in the intricacies
of your brain arena
a demented take-them-on and
make-them-see-dust-messi
reserving my best for moments
such as these
when with mouth agape
you salute with a saliva-drooled
WOW

THOUGHTS

He dreamt his brain
Crept out of his head
Through his astonished eyes
Slithering unhurriedly
Like gooey excretion
Down his indifferent cheeks
It deposited itself
On his lap and there
Sat illuminating him
With frantic thoughts
Whose mesmerizing fingers
Stitched haphazardly
Multi-coloured patches
To cover glaring holes
On his thinking cap
Using his emotions
As thread and his
Ambition as needle

He longed to swat at it
As one would, a fly, kill
And destroy all the smugness
Housed in its grey cells
Where scales
Calibrated to measure
His worth against
Peers, kith & kin
Enjoy pride of place

So he glared at it
With stabbing looks
That perforated its exterior
And entered its core
And there surprised he
Truth and myth

Sitting entwined in
Easy copulation
Striving to conceive
A child of nameless pedigree
One that neither hungers
Breathes nor dies

CALENDAR

Here, days abide
Imprisoned in paper cells
And locked in place
By padlocks of ink
I look at them
And wonder
At their stoic loyalty
In staying at their
Allotted station without
Deviation day by day.

They got tales to tell
Some sad some tall
Some about the day
Mother missed her period
And she came and
Stared and stared
At them
As if willing them
To go back to those times
When the plumber
Was not such a temptation
And father was not such a brute

They tell too tales
Of the day
When in silence
Sister came high
On illicit substances,
Circled the day's date
And began to mutter that
As long as she had time
On her hands
She could weave it

How ever she chose;
And in that instance
Her wrists, she
immediately slit

And as the life
Ebbed out of her,
She saw the dates
Looking at her
Without surprise
And with the smug look
Of one who is
On talking terms with fate
And knows beforehand
Each footprint imprinted
On the beach of tomorrow,

And knows too the
Exact moment in time
When a wave shall
From the seas emerge
And obliterate all
Traces of trails walked
Upon the sands of time.....

TAKEN

Passion is a gun
Whose trigger is caressed by the emotions
The deafening blast and ardent spit
Is the disgusted expletive
Of the pure in man
But this unlikely love
Sired by cold steel and explosive gunpowder
And consummated in the blued gut of the bullet chamber
With death targeting the heart gleefully along eager barrel
Defies circumstance, form and time
In the demon infested gun powder fumes
Where weeping, teeth-gnashing butchered souls abound
Your huntress' instinct sweetly unhinges my resolve
And in the magical never-never land of your mouth
I discover to the completion of my doom
That elixir and the forbidden fruit
Are mutually exclusive treats

WEDDING NIGHT

let love whisper a serenade
coaxed from the wind's
breathless symphony
and seduce the rainbow
with the dainty giggles
of rose tickled faeries
sweetly disrobing it
of its virginal robes
of mating colors
to adorn the bride's
bashful innocence
for the honeymoon altar

EPITAPH

His fate was writ in water
Penned by the wind
In its gentler moments
Abhorring the salty destination
That awaited him
In the seas of commonality
He departed
Silently with vapour stealth
Leaving his legacy hanging angrily
Like stormy clouds
Threatening to burst torrentially
And create oases of hope
In the deserts of our mourning

LEAVING HOME

This road today
I know we walked it
Before in times
When it pointed to
Horizons unexplored
Where rainbows
Mated with sunsets
To bring to life
A world so dreamy
And tantalizing
A world so enticing
That we forgot
The pain of trekking
And the sweet call
Of mother's voice
As she hummed that
Ageless hymn
Whilst coaxing the
Tired soils that
Now refused to nourish
Even the hardiest seed
And yet day to day
To that field she
Her way she faithfully made
To fulfil the undying pact
That she had
With the rains made
To dig graves for
It's aborted droplets
Who fall to this earth
To gift life
A chance at life

HEAVEN

Where now to turn to
And seek sanity
In a world where truth
Is found hidden
In the undergarments
Of a harlot adorning
A nun's habit on
Snapchat and Instagram

The televangelist
Wears mini skirts
Preaching a gospel
Rinsed of divine aura
To a congregation that
Throngs in week after week
For a hopeful glimpse
Of the outline of the fruit
That Eve leafily covered

Father already has
His heaven figured
It smells of hops and barley
And stays imprisoned
In its metal can
Till he liberates it
Only to promptly consign it
To the gallows in his gut

But I love mother's
heaven the most
It smells of father
And earthen floors
And smoky fires
And damp mud
In the midst of drought

FATHER'S DAY

He became a father
One drunken day
When the club spotlights
Connived with the cheeky mascara
And naughty lipstick
To carve a stunning beauty
Out of mother's poverty
Ravaged face

I tell you
He became a father
Somewhere in the back alleys
Of frontline brothels
Where orgasms are metered
And pleasure is counterfeit
And condoms pronounced reusable
Only to burst in protest
Showering seed into
Unprepared fields
But fertile all the same

He became a father
On a day when alcohol
Stole his memory
And rendered him comatose
And so to his shirtless
Wandering he retired
To wake up the morrow
Without recollection of
The arable land he had ploughed
And the seed he had planted

Today mother frequents
Still the same bar

will not increase this year. I am in my bedroom where once again, my fragment of fierce joy is somehow wrong for who and where I am. Here I am not a comrade, even a white one. Here I am the white girlfriend of a man who is afraid of the men with cricket bats. He has asked me to stay with him. I cannot refuse.

For two shining days then, as the country's 'flesh-coloured' Band-aids are ripped from the story we tell ourselves to get to sleep, he hid in my home. How could I say aloud that those two days were the most time we'd had together in months, and so I was happy? He was there and my body welcomed me with unusually juicy joy. It found itself to be, surprisingly, alive.

Now, he has arrived after three months apart. I know the bedrock has long moved, old cracks opening beneath our feet. How to stretch our worn love across an African border, with data charges and familial pressures, now we are done with this bewildering place.

But he is arriving and I am giddy with love, despite all. My degree is conferred, the one I almost abandoned when the ghosts of a dark house in a dark town threaded over my mouth as they tear-gassed my friends and told me not to speak. He shopped for me with my mother's money and I ate him as safety. I believe he is in the room, as I am capped and they tell me I have crossed the contour of a finishing line to somewhere.

He is not. He has chosen not to be, and it is done.

I am 19 when he first touches me - as though I am wondrous. I am 23 when he holds me for the final time, his father - who I imagined he'd resemble when we were old together on a stoep in the vision he painted - watching benignly and teasing he'll mail him across the Orange River to be with me again. How like him to not have told his father that today's goodbye is the last, a strangely peaceful postscript to yesterday's calamity as he pulls me from the aftermath of the ceremony where I am anointed top Political & International Studies student on what should be a triumphant day. I wear my ankara dresses and, unusually, feel beautiful – lean with pain – as I smile and stumble over the word boyfriend introducing him to the department head who has materialised. His dad is plump with pride. How like him not to have told him. So here I sit, as he holds my hand, we pose for photographs and I reach for smiles I would have refuted as unthinkable – emblematic of a future we all want to imagine, the love of a young white South African Afrikaans woman committed to political emancipation and a young black Namibian Oshivambo man who is bringing a degree home to his hard-working parents. For a moment, it was.

But here I am, with the quiet knowledge my heart is seeping down my thighs into my specially bought sensible wedge heels.

Suddenly, he cannot bear it – the looming loss – and pulls me from this bafflingly sunny place into the shade of the Philosophy Department bench where we sat the night we met. He doesn't want to let go. I am afraid his grip is going to shatter the spine I have constructed to keep standing through this day.

Later, when the longing is drowning my lungs, I call him to say none of it matters. We can chart a path back to the beginning. I can live in a town lacking fruit or books. I can continue to carve myself out. It doesn't matter what that final time was like – flung from the young and glistening ones who let his parents feast on my first university marks; who had eaten celebratory pizza gazing forward at the Namibian hills, dripping with glory; who touched each other where we'd never been touched before.

68

I want to be them so badly it leaks out of the scar on my hand from that day – when I sat holding myself still in the café, after the barista called his name. I hold myself a glacier, so as not to flood this godforsaken *gat* in the ground, until this ever-unreliable land snaps. I am bleeding from the trunk of my palm and he is bandaging it with such tender grace that it is as though my hand is weeping. Something is echoed in this moment of bowed heads, a prayer to when he cracked open on a bathroom floor – his magnificent runner's limbs all folded in upon each other as he sobbed into the air already heavy with wet. It did not stop for an age, and later I look back on this and see that this is when he knew.

Just as the scar is stitching a vivid blush, someone steals the ring. Reaches into my heart and yanks, for a trinket to flog. It's almost laughable. A cheap pink box - that is what is left of that day, closing her eyes.

* *oppad na die pleknaam toe*: enroute to the place's name (Afrikaans)
**gat*: hole (Afrikaans)

In-hail

Although it isn't said aloud,
smoking a cigarette on your stone stoep
on the morning of your mother's 62nd birthday
can be an act of emotional maturity.

A childhood clouded in others' lungs
as my two small lurid pink calliopes hold their breath

now, I expand into adulthood
as Eva Ernst's claws contract from my oesophagus.

This nicotine is my choice.

Exhale

Men

I gave you all a small wounded heart had.

I allowed you to strip me until I didn't feel clean.

I needed you to tell me when I was lovely.

I shook at the touch of your mind.

I held your hand after it crushed me.

I cracked my own ribs breathing you all out.

He Left me by the Hand

It appears as a thought
Wholly formed
not oven-ready as Johnson spews
but quietly whole
pregnant goose
I didn't know was nesting all along

I'm sorry you love me.
I believe that you do, to my bemusement
But, for you, wish you did not.

"Love is a dangerous word"
the conman warns the mermaid
which am I?

My husband doesn't have cruel in him
even when he drinks
which is often.
Even when I am quaking
with rage at having to recall a miner's terror,
he cannot be woken except to say how pretty I am.

My bigoted boss warns me with sincerity
woman needs a shark's egg of cash
buried beneath an unremarkable dune
for bolting.

I'm lousy at running
all that genetic smog
but I've been seeing the only other man to ever enter me
in the shape of people's ears

and remembering his phalanges in the night.

He couldn't take it either
the chemical shadows of childhood.

I remember the final time he slithered from my cervix
I knew then -
it didn't matter what promises we'd made years before in that same
bed
in a haze of Namibian heat and faith in Freedom Day's symmetry.

So today the thought comes
how would I leave my husband
how would I hide myself from him
in a country always more his than mine
no matter how much I pay or study
for one of those filmic acts of nobility I loath
where you decide for them how much grief they can hold.

A Love Poem

The month we met
I discovered a cookie recipe
made for 65 Catholics
swallowed by greasy teenagers –

I didn't notice.
I was looking at you.

Once

I caught a bus in the gloom today.
The hospital wasn't my stop.

Once,
I rode taut silence
to the hospital where my mother radiated her chest.
They dyed her to the soundtrack of Adele.

It is distinct
from the one sainted
with birth, that of my mother,
stiefma, brother, sister,
and mine.

They poured water through me,
in a skin-thin gown
in a hollow room
to wash me clean
to see my womb.

The nurses clucked their frowns
because I brought a man inside –
it's his bloody contraception too.

stiefma: stepmother (Afrikaans)

Diagnosis

You made me smile
until it belonged to you.

Then, when I did not smile at all
doctors dripped diagnoses.

It is simple —
I am striving to re-claim my face
                       my flippancy
                       my fuck
                       my flesh.

Friday's Absence

On Monday, I told the man who waited a year to make
love to me that I remember his soul/on Tuesday, I told
another who stroked my palm in Grade 9 Natural Science,
he lies beside me in my dreams at 25/listened as another
told me he's loved me since he asked me to tutor him in
Philosophy/on Wednesday, I asked another why he
touched my hair while dating her/listened as he told me he
remembers me comfortably nude at 16/never saw an
object when he looked at me/asked me to teach him how
to be naked in the sea/on Thursday I read the letter saying
he remembers mine too.

Fifteenth

I am nothing. The gentle filter-cloth of the mosquito net
that traps me,
sparing the world my bloodsucking sting has been crisped
away.

Hold me goddamnit. Do I ever ask you to think?
If I coated, painted, rolled onto the teeth of the world my
coagulating conflabulating sticky red blood,
would it stop?

Why weren't you holding me already? That's what
womanhood is like -
the pink fluffy bits fall out of you in clots of a red dark
enough to be black and still gleam.
You don't taste nice.
If I open my mouth and eat the world, would I tear tuna
biltong, sing caffeine and vomit through my eyes?
A little girl hates her body because it demands she wear
pants so that she doesn't bleed on the floor
while 'her' society throws rocks of old grey clay.

Why does she not hate them
instead?

From One Ward Patient to Another

I hope the tea lady makes juicy *rooibos*.

I hope the vegetables know colour.

I hope the shower stops your waters breaking.

I hope the therapy room knows light when it sees it.

I hope the crayons rub you in.

I hope the blood-taker laughs, with warmth, to open your veins.

I hope the coffee shop serves sweet potato *slap tjips*.

But most of all...I was there.
Still...I hope.

The Spring

When that which is unbearable

ends

a body

political/physical/personal

unbends

breathes

the World

again.

The Hysterical Girl

The doctor tells me that the medication they are giving me for my brain is affecting my breasts.

The misogynist argues it's the having of the breasts in the first place that screwed my brain.

I'm breastfeeding non-existent babies and breathing into bags.

Oh! That's why he calls me hysterical.

Hands

It's the hands.

That's what I recall.

Of each of those I have loved.

They are individual in a way that mouths are not.

Nursing

My eardrums ache/in the psychiatric ward/my stomach
roils/the blonde *boere-poppie* with red lipstick on her nurse's
uniform tries to administer help/but her mascara has
stretched her eye too bright/ besides, that's not the kind
of pain for which they lock you in.

*boere-poppie: Afrikaans doll

See Jane Run

I read Jane Eyre at 16
like a good white girl.
But I related
not to Jane
that pale facsimile of a woman
but to the wife
the burning woman
locked in the attic
haunting the halls
tearing bridal veils
screeching her rage.

In Response to Japan Pumps Seawater into Nuclear Reactor Unit

I tried to recall the sensation of 'cold' from the long years spent at the pole. All that flooded my body was the sensation of being frozen, unable to dance, leap, stream – held twixt one moment and the next, for centuries.
And then the sound came.

When I lay still, in my liquid form, my family around me, we lay quiet. When we moved, we could feel sound in our bodies – roaring and pouring.
When something moved in the ice, there was a cracking and then a trickling, deep down –

I felt that too.

Freed from the ice, we danced and flowed again, rejoicing and celebrating in the Great Sun.
Our liberator – from still to slip and slip to sky.
We raced to be the surface drops that felt and knew His heat, so energized, so rapid, His touch thrilling.
Nature met nature in exciting, slick foreplay.
Would He leave us to the calm, chilling presence of the moon, leave us before he took us up?
Would He leave me before his wonderful heat touched every particle and let me rise, conjoined, enraptured, of the air?
I chased this, even as I danced – forward, forward – enjoying the rapture of being again part of the moving wave.

And now I tried to recall the sensation of 'cold.' Rapidly. Desperately. I tried to recall opening myself to Him; to Heat. To recall flowing forward, pre-empting rolling, rushing, wanting the crashing, delighting in the friction of crest and crashed.

Now there was only movement, only heat.
We crashed together, roared together, poured together. The wave brought us closer, closer, a rising swell, that continued to rise, continued to swell, on, on, – forward, forward – until the frontline touched it, felt it, cringed – tried to drift, even flow, back, down - from that unbearable heat. We rolled them on in the tide, as we always had. They met it, were energized by it, touched, each caress brought climax, so close was the source of this heat. This was no Sun, there was no foreplay, no thrilling, no distance, no yearning. The dark heat thrust us, from slip to sky, without delicious delay. But sky, sky was a space with no light, no freedom, the sky here knew an acme.

And still we rushed on.

And still I tried to recall the sensation of 'cold.'

The Second Election

Is it immoral, apolitical even
to beg God
for safety
when themselves
state: safe is not the same
as whole.

Three Weeks

I weep like a person is dead
when the new bud of a small cacti
bought in a pretty, racist town
with love and irony rots.

22

God texts me lime-pink ash to chisel grief into bite-sized
bits,
clot the voice met fynbos as, popping dog-eared dusty
purple bubbles of pain.

There are no new words for

abandoned.

Ugly-lonely
the joker dis-card
gutted
peeled
pinned
forgot.

A frayed gold-pink doily
dyed white like dirt
beetroot meat like yellow hairy rage I misplaced
roasting in 22 centimetres of shame.

A Year Ago

I was in love. I wore a chain around my neck to prove it.

I was so tired I couldn't see. It wasn't still on the surface like it is now. I was moving, dodging, running. There were stairs in my house and they taught me why one says "I took the stairs." It's aggressive, expressive. That damned house. It was dark when I arrived, heavy with other people and not happy ones at that. There was a steak knife in my room, cheap and flimsy, a pot, and a half-drunk cooldrink. Dank and rank, the place felt like the set of a horror. I pulled joy out of that place, link by link. Hanging laundry in the backyard, I could never find the pegs I had bought for the house, except for the broken bits in the grass that was somehow always wet. I took pictures, partly for records for the landlord, partly in shock, as if to prove to myself it was as frightening as it felt. It loomed, that house - such a contrast to the year before, when my boyfriend and I were first to arrive at the digs. It wasn't welcoming in any real sense of the word. It was dirty, and unkempt. He spent a morning disinfecting the oven while I wrote an exam, and there was a blissful moment when I knew what it was to make a home and have someone in it who loves you. We sat on a mattress, careful to keep our toes on the too-small sheet. There were broken things then too, but we were whole, for one of the last times and so, slick as it sounds, their b

rokenness mattered less.

Still I tried, to forge something new in the looming place. I bought a bathmat from PEP, and spent a Friday evening decorating the cupboards that ate up all the space. I was forever finding people's leftovers in those cupboards, some disturbing. I kept only the stationery, filling black bag after black bag with stuff in the true sense of the word – dusty, cloistered, sticky, discards that clog and close. I think it was September when I found the last of it. I hung lace in the window like in Enid Blyton tree-houses, and draped the house in cloths from Lome, Kinshasa and Accra.

I had done the same in Accra once. Arrived to a place of cupboards unopened, surfaces uncleaned, corners untouched. Volunteers arrived and left, leaving little but for their discards. That's how it felt. A place made up of long-gone transitory occupants' discards. I took a weekend and scrubbed, opened, tried to let some light in. I created a little library of volunteers' books, and found objects even the owners had forgotten. It felt more like mine after that.

This place didn't. This place held on to its air of discardedness until long after I arrived. It was a matter of small victories and small spaces I carved out as mine. My bathroom, which after some months finally had a door handle, was mine, with its shells, pink towels and messy pile of laundry. Hozier's *Angel of Small Death* and *Arsonist's Lullaby* still evoke a luke-warm afternoon bath in a room of pale pink tiles.

Sitting with my breakfast on the back porch in drowning pyjamas, the ribbons of my green birthday balloons

92

fluttering where the roof would reach if there was one; rolled into the blanket I crocheted, drinking crass rosé wine and reading history as looming as my house at the imposing dining room table with Size; watching people visiting the restaurant of stodgy pizzas across the road out my window; watching *Charmed* on my magnificently wide bed which took up more room than there was and kept my thighs in bruised shape; communal moments in the grimy kitchen and cluttered and cold dining room.

It was a hideous place when I arrived; a haunting place when I left, 10 months later. But in that time, there was a moment when I'd come home and someone was cooking dinner; or I opened the peephole and he was there, too tall for it by half; or someone was baking; or a digs mate knocked on my door unexpectedly. There was a moment, when I could offer food or tea to someone; when we always had coffee and gherkins; when Peter made spaghetti bolognaise like clockwork; when my bathroom was clean, that my performance of being at home didn't feel false.

I never remembered if I had locked the door. I always had. I hated that house, even the day I made two chicken pies and a rice salad. I was ashamed of it when my dad came for dinner, and I made jollof rice with brown rice that wouldn't go soft. But there was an evening my parents and my boyfriend's parents came to that house after graduation. There'd been many ceremonies that day. I stripped off my heels and cleaned that room in 10 minutes. When they arrived that looming room was made welcoming by my cloths and candlelight, and the wine being drunk from my mugs and the girls doing the drinking had been shuffled off. There was a moment then, with my mom and dad in the same room, and his parents, and my brother, and speech made soft by pride and relief bubbling below the civility, I didn't feel false then.

That was before. Before I took off the chain, and started wearing the ring; before I demonstrated the flimsiness of that life by packing it up in a single day; before another graduation came and went with pain that peculiar mix of excruciating and numb, like when a bandage is yanked clear; before the hospital. That was before I realised the house was a sign of things to come. That was before I realised what was looming. That was before, but I suppose, it also was.

Rusted Pride

I climb into a rusted-out Ford pick-up truck. I was 18, just.
A sarcastically handsome man is driving. Here is Brother 1,
blonde spiky hair, toned and tanned, blue-eyed … Norse
even. His mother's name is Eva – a name she shares with
my ancestor Krotoa van die Kaap. What peculiar root
systems have embedded into this strange land of ours …
James Phillips/Bernoldus Niemand sings 'All these foreign
ideas are just a waste of time in this land of mine.' But he is
playing with the word foreign, rolling it around on his
tongue and holding it in his left cheek as I have learned to
do. Here is Brother 1, named for an angel. His energy is
tough, but he finds me vaguely entertaining. Mostly, he is
bemused – almost angry – that with nothing but his
mother's voice on the telephone and a vague notion of
where their dairy farm is in the Tsitsikama mountain range,
I have climbed into his car. He's not wrong and is relieved
when I say it aloud in the tiny cab that I know it is a bizarre,
even dangerous, act. But I am chafing to be in the world,
and my depression has been monstrous. So for five hours,
that become eight because of roadworks, we are bonded in
his car – which is a strong word for something more rust
than metal. It is dark when we reach the final mountains, a
different dark to the cities where night time is always tinted
orange. We are winding around a terror-fying road, high on
the slopes. There is no barrier between us and the earth at
the base of the valley - only a kilometre of air sweating rain
out into the night. We know it is there, a gap, and the car
huddles against the mountainside but the rain has made the
roads slick. We are going fast, too fast, around the hips and

breasts of this ancient place. Were the headlamps not glinting off raindrops for a primary school ruler's distance, we'd just be floating fast as there is no lamp inside the car. Me, this man, a few layers of oxidised metal, asking the earth, will we die?

I remember the moon. Lying on the back of another pick-up truck, seated opposite another brother. Brother 2 is different, an iteration of how Jesus is portrayed by the white world. He is bearded, with kindly and sparking eyes. Thin and tall, paler than his brother despite working on the farm. He likes to talk with me, intellectually starved for company I think. We write letters after I leave the farm – pages of neat blue words. He plays the violin. Brother 1 plays the piano – in his small hutch building emblematic of his rebellion from his parents' isolated life. There is no electricity on the farm, and no hot water without making a fire. But Brother 1 has a small generator for the tiny white structure where he plays the piano and smokes, while Brother 2 tuts disapprovingly in the dark old stone house. The father is frightening, so I don't remember his name. Mostly he is just quiet, but his presence is large. But one night, as we discuss music around the table by candlelight and eat the crunchy warm bread we have baked that day with goat's cheese from the goats we have milked, he speaks up suddenly – that there was one musician he saw who he has never forgotten. He had radiant talent and a rare name – so in his case, he has remembered it all these years. And he spoke my father's stage name out into the quiet hum of a single lit room in the dark. Hanepoot van Tonder. And I, still aching with homesickness despite choosing to leave barely a few days before, am nourished as I say quietly in Afrikaans, 'Dis *my pa.*' Little of my father belongs to me, even less in those days when I needed more, so this gentle moment of pride shines inside of me for years as a candle lit again and again by parishioners.

Dis my pa: That's my dad (Afrikaans)

Two Geese

O friend, when you go to Gao make a detour by Timbuktu &
murmur my name to my friends & bring them a greeting perfumed
with an exile that yearns after the soil where its friends, family &
neighbours reside – Ahmed Baba al-Timbukti

In my land of home
I flinch from birds
see only sharp beaks and talon hands
baby brother's Indian myna, named for a pirate, spits "fuck you"
and stalks me
reaching for my trembling feet's soft souls
everyone crows at his verbosity
until he slits my mother's cheekbone.

Her baby brother says, "it means he likes you"
what they tell the little girl when a boy first hurts her

But in a land of swanning falsehood
adoration folds from me
to the frantic ducklings and ungainly moorhens,
the graciously lethal heron

I am enchanted by Canadian geese
she nesting in shade
he quietly on guard
making still life
I join him daily, a second sentry,
until the spell cracks open
three yellow fluffy prayers
so foreign to their parents' chic

I no longer flinch from birds
I see bodies moulded for flight
lifting into the wide sky
swallow your gavel Home Secretary
parents pairing for life
pillows of babies nestling together

mother goose ate from my hand once,

Unafraid &
Free.

The Secret of this Loving

The secret of this loving can be found on a bench in a city we no longer live in.

It is quiet and vivid, midst a storm of grit.

It is we, bearing witness to the Divine, in watching the two geese in the pond at the park that you named Gertrude & Humphrey grow birth three clumsy, soft goslings midst London's mania. She nests, as he guards – never crowding, never straying. They hatch, learn to glide upon their wet, moving landscape & ultimately to fly as giant birds of the sky…

That is where I find the secret to this loving on days when the world is a sack of sand, silently watching the wondrous with you.

It is in the wild swimming at Tinside East, where you leap without pause and promptly get out, as I tentatively adapt body part at a time and stay to float as my granny did. You wait on the shore, never rushing & regardless of how deep I swim, I am safe because you are there.

The secret to this love in the truth-telling – the labour of communicating each day, tending each other gently, even when anger rolls.

It is in the silly, the laughing, the naming of the vacuum cleaner.

The secret of this loving is in being put to bed with a kiss on my forehead, soothed by the roars of AEW dynamite in the lounge. It is in your ability to give me space, with your hand at my back.

The secret of this loving is an honour to behold.

It is unwavering, dedicated, insightful, brilliant.

The secret of this loving is you.

Mmap New African Poets Series

If you have enjoyed *a sky is falling*, consider these other fine books in the **New African Poets** Series from *Mwanaka Media and Publishing:*

I Threw a Star in a Wine Glass by Fethi Sassi
Best New African Poets 2017 Anthology by Tendai R Mwanaka and Daniel Da Purificacao
Logbook Written by a Drifter by Tendai Rinos Mwanaka
Mad Bob Republic: Bloodlines, Bile and a Crying Child by Tendai Rinos Mwanaka
Zimbolicious Poetry Vol 1 by Tendai R Mwanaka and Edward Dzonze
Zimbolicious Poetry Vol 2 by Tendai R Mwanaka and Edward Dzonze
Zimbolicious: An Anthology of Zimbabwean Literature and Arts, Vol 3 by Tendai Mwanaka
Under The Steel Yoke by Jabulani Mzinyathi
Fly in a Beehive by Thato Tshukudu
Bounding for Light by Richard Mbuthia
Sentiments by Jackson Matimba
Best New African Poets 2018 Anthology by Tendai R Mwanaka and Nsah Mala
Words That Matter by Gerry Sikazwe
The Ungendered by Delia Watterson
Ghetto Symphony by Mandla Mavolwane
Sky for a Foreign Bird by Fethi Sassi
A Portrait of Defiance by Tendai Rinos Mwanaka
Zimbolicious: An Anthology of Zimbabwean Literature and Arts, Vol 4 by Tendai Mwanaka and Jabulani Mzinyathi
When Escape Becomes the only Lover by Tendai R Mwanaka
ويَسهَرُ اللَّيلُ عَلى شَفَتي...وَالغَمَام by Fethi Sassi
A Letter to the President by Mbizo Chirasha
This is not a poem by Richard Inya

102

Pressed flowers by John Eppel
Righteous Indignation by Jabulani Mzinyathi:
Blooming Cactus By Mikateko Mbambo
Rhythm of Life by Olivia Ngozi Osouha
Travellers Gather Dust and Lust by Gabriel Awuah Mainoo
Chitungwiza Mushamukuru: An Anthology from Zimbabwe's Biggest Ghetto Town by Tendai Rinos Mwanaka
Zimbolicious: An Anthology of Zimbabwean Literature and Arts, Vol 5 by Tendai Mwanaka
Because Sadness is Beautiful? by Tanaka Chidora
Of Fresh Bloom and Smoke by Abigail George
Shades of Black by Edward Dzonze
Best New African Poets 2020 Anthology by Tendai Rinos Mwanaka, Lorna Telma Zita and Balddine Moussa
This Body is an Empty Vessel by Beaton Galafa
Between Places by Tendai Rinos Mwanaka
Best New African Poets 2021 Anthology by Tendai Rinos Mwanaka, Lorna Telma Zita and Balddine Moussa
Zimbolicious: An Anthology of Zimbabwean Literature and Arts, Vol 6 by Tendai Mwanaka and Chenjerai Mhondera
A Matter of Inclusion by Chad Norman
Keeping the Sun Secret by Mariel Awendit
سِجلٌّ مَكْتُوبٌ لثَائِهِ by Tendai Rinos Mwanaka
Ghetto Blues by Tendai Rinos Mwanaka
Zimbolicious: An Anthology of Zimbabwean Literature and Arts, Vol 7 by Tendai Rinos Mwanaka and Tanaka Chidora
Best New African Poets 2022 Anthology by Tendai Rinos Mwanaka and Helder Simbad
Dark Lines of History by Sithembele Isaac Xhegwana

Soon to be released

Along the Way by Jabulani Mzinyathi
Strides of Hope by Tawanda Chigavazira
Death of a statue by Samuel Chuma
The politics of Life by Mandhla Mavolwane

https://facebook.com/MwanakaMediaAndPublishing/

Printed in the United States
by Baker & Taylor Publisher Services